What to do with my business after I'm dead

Notebook for recording my business details and instructions on how to deal with everything after I die

Keep Track Books

CreateSpace, Charleston SC
Design © Keep Track Books

All rights reserved
No part of this publication may be reproduced, stored in a retrieval system, or transmitted in any form or by any means, electronic, mechanical, photocopying, recording or otherwise, without the prior written permission of the copyright owner.

Unauthorised reproduction of any part of this publication by any means including photocopying is an infringement of copyright.

Contents

Introduction	5
My personal details	7
Basic details of the business	8
Business partners	9
Shareholders & other people with significant control	10
Companies House	12
Tax affairs — Self-assessment	13
Tax affairs — Corporation tax	14
Tax affairs — VAT	15
Tax affairs — Tax on foreign income	16
Tax affairs — Other tax information	17
Important contact details	18
Important documents & where to find them	20
Banking details — Bank accounts	23
Banking details — Credit, debit and store cards	26
Income	29
Customers	36
Outgoings	40
Suppliers	42
Loans that the business owes	46
Loans that are owed to the business	48
Employees	49
PAYE & payroll details	52
Insurance	53
Business premises	56
Other property	57
Vehicles	59
Equipment	61
Intellectual property	65
Business storage	68
What beneficiaries can expect	70

Utilities	72
Memberships	76
Subscriptions	78
Online accounts	80
Email, website and social media	84
Miscellaneous details not covered elsewhere	87
If I am not able to communicate, I would like the following to be known	92
What to do with my business	93
People who know about this book	100
Additional notes	101

Introduction

This is a notebook for recording your business details as well as your wishes with regard to what should happen to your business after you pass away or if you are ever in a situation where you are not able to express your wishes. It will be a valuable guide for people who are left behind so that they will know what to do and how to look after your business affairs.

How to use this notebook

Fill in as many details as you can. The more information those who are left behind have, the easier it will be for them to respect your wishes and arrange things in a way that you would like.

Whenever you come across a section that doesn't apply to your business, you can either draw a dash (—) or leave the area blank. If any aspects of your business or your wishes are not covered, use the additional space at the back of the book to record those. You can also insert extra pages if you need more space. However, remember to attach them securely so that they won't get lost.

You don't have to finish writing all your business information and wishes in one go, so take as much time as you need.

Once you have recorded all the details, store this notebook in a safe place (for example, with your solicitor or in a safe).

You may need to update this notebook from time to time. If the circumstances change or if you want to change your wishes, remember to update those details.

It's a good idea to tell your business partners/close family/friends about the existence of this notebook and where you keep it. This way they will know where to look for it when you pass away.

**Please note that this book is not a will or a legal document.
It does <u>not</u> replace a will.**

Other helpful things to do

❧ Make a will. This book is not a legal document so it cannot be used as a substitute for a will.

❧ Set up Power of Attorney. This is a legal document that allows another person to make decisions for you, or act on your behalf, if you are not able to do this yourself or if you no longer wish to make your own decisions.

❧ Make sure you communicate your personal information and wishes to your loved ones so that they will know what to do with your personal affairs after you are gone. You can use a book similar to this one called *Gone but not forgotten: What to do after I'm dead* to record these details. To find out more, visit www.lusciousbooks.co.uk/gone-but-not-forgotten.

> Find out more about wills and Power of Attorney:
>
> GOV.UK (UK government website)
> www.gov.uk
>
> Citizens Advice
> www.citizensadvice.org.uk
>
> Age UK
> www.ageuk.org.uk

❧ Record all your business contact details in an address book/your computer/online address book/app and keep the information updated.

❧ If your business has many online accounts, record all the account details and passwords in a separate notebook. It will be easier to keep that notebook updated as opposed to using this one. You can find specifically designed password notebooks at www.lusciousbooks.co.uk/password-notebooks.

❧ Finally, always keep your business records appropriately stored and organised.

Advice to those left behind

This notebook contains wishes and instructions on what to do with my business after I'm gone. When you start dealing with my business affairs, it's a good idea to acquire multiple copies of the death certificate — photocopies of the original are not likely to be accepted everywhere.

My personal details

Full name

Maiden name

Address

I moved to this address on

Previous address

I moved to this address on

Telephone number

Mobile phone number

Email

Date of birth

Place of birth

Next of kin

His/her relationship to me

His/her contact details

Additional notes

Basic details of the business

Business name

___

Type of business

☐ sole trader

☐ limited company

☐ partnership — further details

___

☐ other — further details

___

Company registration number

Date of incorporation

Date the business became active

My role within the business

___

Registered address

___

Summary of what the business does

Business partners

☐ I do not have any business partners

☐ My business partners are

Name

Role

Contact details

Additional notes

Name

Role

Contact details

Additional notes

Name

Role

Contact details

Additional notes

Shareholders & other people with significant control

☐ There are no shareholders or other people with significant control

☐ The shareholders and/or other people with significant control are

Name

Role

Contact details

Details of shares

Additional notes

Name

Role

Contact details

Details of shares

Additional notes

Shareholders & other people with significant control

Name

Role

Contact details

Details of shares

Additional notes

Name

Role

Contact details

Details of shares

Additional notes

Companies House

Company registration number

Company authentication code

Date company became active

Filing of accounts is due by

Confirmation statement (annual return) is due by

☐ Online account details can be found in the password notebook

☐ Online account details are as follows

Paperwork relating to Companies House is located

Additional notes

Tax affairs — Self-assessment

☐ The business pays income tax via self-assessment

National insurance number

Unique taxpayer reference (UTR)

Accounting period

☐ Online account details can be found in the password notebook

☐ Online account details are as follows

Paperwork relating to self-assessment is located

Additional notes

Tax affairs — Corporation tax

☐ The business pays corporation tax

Company unique taxpayer reference (UTR)

Office number

Accounting period

☐ Online account details can be found in the password notebook

☐ Online account details are as follows

Paperwork relating to corporation tax is located

Additional notes

Tax affairs — VAT

☐ My business is not VAT registered

☐ My business is VAT registered

VAT registration number

Effective date of registration

Direct debit reference

Scheme type

VAT return due date(s)

☐ Online account details can be found in the password notebook

☐ Online account details are as follows

VAT paperwork is located

Additional notes

Tax affairs — Tax on foreign income

Details of tax on foreign income

Tax affairs — Other tax information

Details of other tax matters

Important contact details

Executor of my will

Name

Contact details

Solicitor

Name

Contact details

Services provided to the business

Accountant

Name

Contact details

Services provided to the business

Important contact details

Other important contact details

Name/role

Contact details

Services provided to the business

Name/role

Contact details

Services provided to the business

Name/role

Contact details

Services provided to the business

Important documents & where to find them

☐ I have not made a will

☐ I have made a will and it contains details relating to my business. My will is located

The business paperwork is located

Additional notes

Important documents & where to find them

☐ All the business contacts can be found in the business address book which is located

☐ All the business contacts are stored on the computer/online and are located

☐ All the business contacts are stored elsewhere — where?

☐ All the business related passwords can be found in the password notebook which is located

☐ All the business related passwords are stored on the computer/online and are located

☐ All the business related passwords are stored elsewhere — where?

Additional notes

Important documents & where to find them

Details of documents and information stored on the computer and/or online

_____
_____
_____
_____
_____
_____
_____
_____
_____
_____
_____
_____
_____
_____
_____
_____
_____

My computer/laptop/tablet passwords

☐ can be found in the password notebook

☐ are as follows

_____
_____

Banking details — Bank accounts

Bank/building society name

Address

Account name

Account type

Sort code/BIC or SWIFT code

Account number/IBAN

Online banking details

☐   can be found in the password notebook

☐   are as follows

Details of direct debits/standing orders/other transactions automatically scheduled to come out of this account

Additional notes

Banking details — Bank accounts

Bank/building society name

Address

Account name

Account type

Sort code/BIC or SWIFT code

Account number/IBAN

Online banking details

☐ can be found in the password notebook

☐ are as follows

Details of direct debits/standing orders/other transactions automatically scheduled to come out of this account

Additional notes

Banking details — Bank accounts

Bank/building society name

Address

Account name

Account type

Sort code/BIC or SWIFT code

Account number/IBAN

Online banking details

☐ can be found in the password notebook

☐ are as follows

Details of direct debits/standing orders/other transactions automatically scheduled to come out of this account

Additional notes

Banking details — Credit, debit and store cards

Card type

Name on the card

Card number

PIN

Online account details

☐ can be found in the password notebook

☐ are as follows

Additional notes

Card type

Name on the card

Card number

PIN

Online account details

☐ can be found in the password notebook

☐ are as follows

Additional notes

Banking details — Credit, debit and store cards

Card type

Name on the card

Card number

PIN

Online account details

☐ can be found in the password notebook

☐ are as follows

Additional notes

Card type

Name on the card

Card number

PIN

Online account details

☐ can be found in the password notebook

☐ are as follows

Additional notes

Banking details — Credit, debit and store cards

Card type

Name on the card

Card number

PIN

Online account details

☐ can be found in the password notebook

☐ are as follows

Additional notes

Card type

Name on the card

Card number

PIN

Online account details

☐ can be found in the password notebook

☐ are as follows

Additional notes

Income

Sales of products
___

The paperwork is located

Income

Services provided

The paperwork is located

Income

Shares and other business investments

The paperwork is located

Income

Commissions

The paperwork is located

Income

Royalties

The paperwork is located

Income

Rental income (e.g. property, land)

_____
_____
_____
_____
_____
_____
_____
_____
_____
_____
_____
_____
_____
_____
_____
_____

The paperwork is located

_____
_____
_____

Income

Other types of income

_____
_____
_____
_____
_____
_____
_____
_____
_____
_____
_____
_____
_____
_____
_____
_____
_____
_____

The paperwork is located

_____
_____
_____
_____

Customers

☐ No customers will need to be contacted when I die.

☐ All customer details can be found in the business address book. I have marked them with this sign _____

☐ All customer details can be found on the computer/online. They are located _____

_____

☐ The customer details are as follows

Name/Business name

_____

Contact details

_____

_____

Additional notes

_____

_____

_____

Name/Business

_____

Contact details

_____

_____

Additional notes

_____

Customers

Name/Business name
_____

_____

Contact details
_____

_____

_____

Additional notes
_____

_____

Name/Business name
_____

_____

Contact details
_____

_____

_____

Additional notes
_____

_____

Name/Business name
_____

_____

Contact details
_____

_____

_____

Additional notes
_____

_____

Customers

Name/Business name
_____
_____

Contact details
_____
_____
_____

Additional notes
_____
_____
_____

Name/Business name
_____
_____

Contact details
_____
_____
_____

Additional notes
_____
_____
_____

Name/Business name
_____
_____

Contact details
_____
_____
_____

Additional notes
_____
_____
_____

Customers

Name/Business name

Contact details

Additional notes

Name/Business name

Contact details

Additional notes

Name/Business name

Contact details

Additional notes

Outgoings

Details of business outgoings

Outgoings

Suppliers

- ☐ No suppliers will need to be contacted when I die.
- ☐ All supplier details can be found in the business address book. I have marked them with this sign
- ☐ All supplier details can be found on the computer/online. They are located

- ☐ The supplier details are as follows

Name/Business name

Contact details

Additional notes

Name/Business

Contact details

Additional notes

Suppliers

Name/Business name

Contact details

Additional notes

Name/Business name

Contact details

Additional notes

Name/Business name

Contact details

Additional notes

Suppliers

Name/Business name

Contact details

Additional notes

Name/Business name

Contact details

Additional notes

Name/Business name

Contact details

Additional notes

Suppliers

Name/Business name

Contact details

Additional notes

Name/Business name

Contact details

Additional notes

Name/Business name

Contact details

Additional notes

Loans that the business owes

Type of loan

Lender's name

Contact details

Loan details

The paperwork is located

Additional notes

Type of loan

Lender's name

Contact details

Loan details

The paperwork is located

Additional notes

Loans that the business owes

Type of loan

Lender's name

Contact details

Loan details

The paperwork is located

Additional notes

Type of loan

Lender's name

Contact details

Loan details

The paperwork is located

Additional notes

Loans that are owed to the business

Type of loan

Borrower's name

Contact details

Loan details

The paperwork is located

Additional notes

Type of loan

Borrower's name

Contact details

Loan details

The paperwork is located

Additional notes

Employees

Name

Job title

Contact details

Additional notes

Name

Job title

Contact details

Additional notes

Name

Job title

Contact details

Additional notes

Employees

Name

Job title

Contact details

Additional notes

Name

Job title

Contact details

Additional notes

Name

Job title

Contact details

Additional notes

Employees

Name

Job title

Contact details

Additional notes

Name

Job title

Contact details

Additional notes

Name

Job title

Contact details

Additional notes

PAYE & payroll details

Employer PAYE reference

Accounts office reference

Accounts office location

PAYE/payroll is administered by

☐ Online account details can be found in the password notebook

☐ Online account details are as follows

PAYE/payroll related paperwork/information is located

Additional notes

Insurance

Type of insurance

Insurer's name

Contact details

Insurance details

The paperwork is located

Additional notes

Type of insurance

Insurer's name

Contact details

Insurance details

The paperwork is located

Additional notes

Insurance

Type of insurance

Insurer's name

Contact details

Insurance details

The paperwork is located

Additional notes

Type of insurance

Insurer's name

Contact details

Insurance details

The paperwork is located

Additional notes

Insurance

Type of insurance

Insurer's name

Contact details

Insurance details

The paperwork is located

Additional notes

Type of insurance

Insurer's name

Contact details

Insurance details

The paperwork is located

Additional notes

Business premises

☐ The premises are owned by the business and the legal paperwork is located
_____
_____

☐ The business is run from my home

☐ The premises are rented and the tenancy agreement is located
_____
_____

Landlord's name and contact details
_____
_____
_____

The keys are located
_____

Building alarm/security details
_____
_____

Other paperwork relating to the business premises is located
_____

Business rates details
_____
_____
_____

Additional notes
_____

Other property

Name of property/land/etc.

Address

Legal documents relating to this property are located

Other paperwork is located

The keys are located

Building alarm/security details

Additional notes

Other property

Name of property/land/etc.

Address

Legal documents relating to this property are located

Other paperwork is located

The keys are located

Building alarm/security details

Additional notes

Vehicles

Vehicle

Make/model/year/colour

Vehicle registration/identification number

Registration paperwork is located

Other paperwork is located

Additional notes

Vehicle

Make/model/year/colour

Vehicle registration/identification number

Registration paperwork is located

Other paperwork is located

Additional notes

Vehicles

Vehicle

Make/model/year/colour

Vehicle registration/identification number

Registration paperwork is located

Other paperwork is located

Additional notes

Vehicle

Make/model/year/colour

Vehicle registration/identification number

Registration paperwork is located

Other paperwork is located

Additional notes

Equipment

Item

This is located

Additional notes

Item

This is located

Additional notes

Item

This is located

Additional notes

Item

This is located

Additional notes

Equipment

Item

This is located

Additional notes

Item

This is located

Additional notes

Item

This is located

Additional notes

Item

This is located

Additional notes

Equipment

Item

This is located

Additional notes

Item

This is located

Additional notes

Item

This is located

Additional notes

Item

This is located

Additional notes

Equipment

Item

This is located

Additional notes

Item

This is located

Additional notes

Item

This is located

Additional notes

Item

This is located

Additional notes

Intellectual property

Details of intellectual property, trademarks, copyright and patents

Intellectual property

Intellectual property

Business storage

Safe

This contains

It is located

The key is located/The combination is

Additional notes

Safety deposit box

This contains

Name of the bank

Address

Box number

The key is located

Additional notes

Business storage

Storage unit(s)

This contains

Name of the storage company

Address and other contact details

Unit number(s)

The key is located

Additional notes

Details of other storage places

What beneficiaries can expect

Details of what beneficiaries can expect

What beneficiaries can expect

Utilities

Name of gas supplier

Account number/details

Contact details

☐ The online account details are recorded in the password notebook

☐ The online account details are as follows

Additional notes

Name of electricity supplier

Account number/details

Contact details

☐ The online account details are recorded in the password notebook

☐ The online account details are as follows

Additional notes

Utilities

Name of oil supplier

Account number/details

Contact details

☐ The online account details are recorded in the password notebook

☐ The online account details are as follows

Additional notes

Name of water supplier

Account number/details

Contact details

☐ The online account details are recorded in the password notebook

☐ The online account details are as follows

Additional notes

Utilities

Name of telephone (landline) provider

Account number/details

Contact details

☐ The online account details are recorded in the password notebook

☐ The online account details are as follows

Additional notes

Name of internet provider

Account number/details

Contact details

☐ The online account details are recorded in the password notebook

☐ The online account details are as follows

Additional notes

Utilities

Name of mobile phone provider

Account number/details

Contact details

☐ The online account details are recorded in the password notebook

☐ The online account details are as follows

Additional notes

Name of provider

Account number/details

Contact details

☐ The online account details are recorded in the password notebook

☐ The online account details are as follows

Additional notes

Memberships

Details of memberships of organisations and associations

Organisation name and contact details

Additional notes

Organisation name and contact details

Additional notes

Organisation name and contact details

Additional notes

Memberships

Organisation name and contact details

Additional notes

Organisation name and contact details

Additional notes

Organisation name and contact details

Additional notes

Subscriptions

Details of subscriptions (e.g. print publications and email newsletters)

Publication name and contact details

_____

_____

_____

Additional notes

_____

_____

_____

Publication name and contact details

_____

_____

_____

Additional notes

_____

_____

_____

Publication name and contact details

_____

_____

_____

Additional notes

_____

_____

_____

Subscriptions

Publication name and contact details

Additional notes

Publication name and contact details

Additional notes

Publication name and contact details

Additional notes

Online accounts

Details of online shopping accounts and other accounts

☐ All the account details are recorded in the password notebook

☐ All the account details are as follows

Website name

Web address

Username

Password

Additional notes

Website name

Web address

Username

Password

Additional notes

Website name

Web address

Username

Password

Additional notes

Online accounts

Website name

Web address

Username

Password

Additional notes

Website name

Web address

Username

Password

Additional notes

Website name

Web address

Username

Password

Additional notes

Website name

Web address

Username

Password

Additional notes

Online accounts

Website name

Web address

Username

Password

Additional notes

Website name

Web address

Username

Password

Additional notes

Website name

Web address

Username

Password

Additional notes

Website name

Web address

Username

Password

Additional notes

Online accounts

Website name

Web address

Username

Password

Additional notes

Website name

Web address

Username

Password

Additional notes

Website name

Web address

Username

Password

Additional notes

Website name

Web address

Username

Password

Additional notes

Emails, website and social media

- ☐ Details relating to business email(s), website(s) and social media account(s) are recorded in the password notebook
- ☐ Details relating to business email(s), website(s) and social media account(s) are as follows

Email

Username

Password

Additional notes

Email

Username

Password

Additional notes

Email

Username

Password

Additional notes

Emails, website and social media

Social media

Username

Password

Additional notes

Social media

Username

Password

Additional notes

Social media

Username

Password

Additional notes

Social media

Username

Password

Additional notes

Emails, website and social media

Website address

Webmaster/administration login details

Domain hosting service and login details

Additional notes

Website address

Webmaster/administration login details

Domain hosting service and login details

Additional notes

Miscellaneous details not covered elsewhere

Miscellaneous details not covered elsewhere

Miscellaneous details not covered elsewhere

Miscellaneous details not covered elsewhere

Miscellaneous details not covered elsewhere

If I am not able to communicate, I would like the following to be known

What to do with my business

☐ I do not mind who deals with my business affairs after I am gone

☐ I would like the following person(s) to look after my business affairs

Name

Contact details

Name

Contact details

Name

Contact details

Additional notes

What to do with my business

My wishes and instructions with regard to what to do with my business

☐ I do not mind what happens to my business after I am gone

☐ I would like my business to be closed — When doing this, please notify/pay/cancel/close/othewise deal with the following:

☐ business partners/shareholders/other people with significant control

☐ solicitor

☐ accountant

☐ bank accounts

☐ credit/debit/store cards

☐ customers

☐ business investments

☐ suppliers

☐ loans owed by the business

☐ loans owed to the business

☐ Companies House

☐ HMRC (self-assessment/corporation tax; VAT; PAYE)

☐ foreign tax affairs

☐ payroll

☐ employees

☐ insurance

☐ business premises (including matters relating to the business rates)

☐ property, vehicles and equipment

☐ business storage

☐ utilities

What to do with my business

- ☐ memberships
- ☐ subscriptions
- ☐ online accounts
- ☐ email account(s)
- ☐ social media account(s)
- ☐ website(s)
- ☐
- ☐
- ☐
- ☐
- ☐
- ☐
- ☐
- ☐
- ☐
- ☐

Additional notes

What to do with my business

☐ I would like my business to continue trading — These are my wishes and instructions with regard to what to do

What to do with my business

What to do with my business

What to do with my business

People who know about this book

Name

Contact details

Name

Contact details

Name

Contact details

Name

Contact details

Additional notes

Additional notes

Additional notes

Keep Track Books brings you a variety of
essential notebooks and journals — including
What to do with my business after I'm dead notebooks
with the same interior as this one, but
with different cover designs.

Please visit www.lusciousbooks.co.uk to find out more.

www.ingramcontent.com/pod-product-compliance
Lightning Source LLC
Chambersburg PA
CBHW082344220526
45470CB00008B/2634